AAT

Advanced Bookkeeping

Pocket Notes

These Pocket Notes support study for the following AAT qualifications:
AAT Advanced Diploma in Accounting – Level 3
AAT Advanced Certificate in Bookkeeping – Level 3
AAT Advanced Diploma in Accounting at SCQF Level 6

British library cataloguing-in-publication data

A catalogue record for this book is available from the British Library.

Published by:
Kaplan Publishing UK
Unit 2 The Business Centre
Molly Millars Lane
Wokingham
Berkshire
RG41 2QZ

ISBN 978-1-78740-817-3

© Kaplan Financial Limited, 2020

Printed and bound in Great Britain.

The text in this material and any others made available by any Kaplan Group company does not amount to advice on a particular matter and should not be taken as such. No reliance should be placed on the content as the basis for any investment or other decision or in connection with any advice given to third parties. Please consult your appropriate professional adviser as necessary. Kaplan Publishing Limited and all other Kaplan group companies expressly disclaim all liability to any person in respect of any losses or other claims, whether direct, indirect, incidental, consequential or otherwise arising in relation to the use of such materials.

Contents

Preface

These Pocket Notes contain the key points you need to know for the exam, presented in a unique visual way that makes revision easy and effective.

Written by experienced lecturers and authors, these Pocket Notes break down content into manageable chunks to maximise your concentration.

Quality and accuracy are of the utmost importance to us so if you spot an error in any of our products, please send an email to mykaplanreporting@kaplan.com with full details, or follow the link to the feedback form in MyKaplan.

Our Quality Co-ordinator will work with our technical team to verify the error and take action to ensure it is corrected in future editions.

A guide to the assessment

The assessment

Advanced Bookkeeping (AVBK) is one of two financial accounting units studied on the Advanced Diploma in Accounting qualification.

Examination

AVBK is assessed by means of a computer based assessment. The CBA will last for 2 hours and consists of 5 tasks.

In any one assessment, students may not be assessed on all content, or on the full depth or breadth of a piece of content. The content assessed may change over time to ensure validity of assessment, but all assessment criteria will be tested over time.

Learning outcomes & weighting

1. Apply the principles of advanced double-entry bookkeeping   24%

2. Implement procedures for the acquisition and disposal of non-current assets   20%

3. Prepare and record depreciation calculations   13%

4. Record period end adjustments   20%

5. Produce and extend the trial balance   23%

Total   100%

Pass mark

To pass a unit assessment, students need to achieve a mark of 70% or more.

This unit contributes 20% of the total amount required for the Advanced Diploma in Accounting qualification.

1

Double entry bookkeeping

- Principles of double entry bookkeeping.
- Accounting equation.
- Ledger accounts.
- General rules of double entry bookkeeping.
- Accounting for cash transactions.
- Accounting for credit transactions.
- Balancing ledger accounts.
- Preparing a trial balance.

Principles of double entry bookkeeping

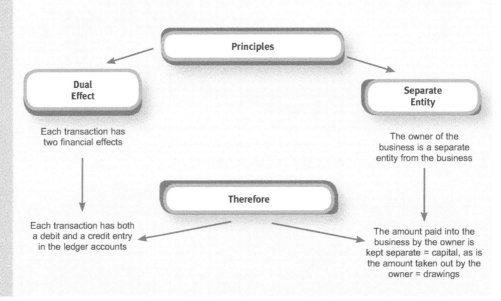

Accounting equation

$$\text{Assets} - \text{Liabilities} = \text{Capital}$$

Terminology

Asset Something owned by the business	**Liability** Something owed by the business	**Capital** Amount the owner has invested in the business	**Receivable** Someone who owes the business money	**Payable** Someone the business owes money to

Ledger accounts

Typical ledger account:

Title of account

Date	Narrative	£	Date	Narrative	£
	Debit side	x		**Credit** side	x

The dual effect means that every transaction is recorded as a debit in one account and a credit in another account.

Key question – which account is the debit entry to and which account is the credit entry to?

General rules of double entry bookkeeping

Ledger account

Debit	Credit
Money in	Money out
Increase in asset	Increase in liability
Decrease in liability	Decrease in asset
Increase in expense	Increase in income

KAPLAN PUBLISHING

Accounting for cash transactions

Examples of ledger accounting:

(i) Payment of £10,000 into business bank account by owner:

Debit Cash (money in)

Credit Capital (increase in liability – amount owed to owner)

Cash account

	£		£
Capital	10,000		

Capital account

	£		£
		Cash	10,000

(ii) Purchase of goods for cash of £3,000:

Debit Purchases (expense)

Credit Cash (money out)

Purchases account

	£		£
Cash	3,000		

Cash account

	£		£
		Purchases	3,000

Accounting for credit transactions

(i) Purchases goods for £6,000 on credit

Debit Purchases (expense)

Credit Trade Payables (liability)

Purchase account

	£		£
Trade payables	6,000		

Trade payables account

	£		£
		Purchases	6,000

(ii) Sale of goods on credit for £8,000

Debit Trade Receivables (asset)

Credit Sales Revenue (income)

Trade receivables account

	£		£
Sales	8,000		

Sales account

	£		£
		Receivables	8,000

(iii) Payment of part of money owed to credit supplier of £1,500

Debit Trade payables (reduction in liability)

Credit Cash (money out)

Trade payables account

	£		£
Cash	1,500		

Cash account

	£		£
		Trade payables	1,500

(iv) Receipt of part of money owed by credit customer of £5,000

Debit Cash (money in)

Credit Trade receivables (reduction in asset)

Cash account

	£		£
Trade receivables	5,000		

Trade receivables account

	£		£
		Cash	5,000

Balancing ledger accounts

At various points in time the owner/owners of a business will need information about the total transactions in the period. Eg, total sales, amount of payables outstanding, amount of cash remaining. This can be found by balancing the ledger accounts.

Here is a typical cash (or bank) account:

Cash account

	£		£
Capital	10,000	Purchases	3,000
Sales	4,000	Rent	500
Receivables	5,000	Payables	1,500

Step 1 Total both debit and credit side and make a note of the totals.

Step 2 Insert higher of totals as total for both sides (leaving a line before inserting totals).

Cash account

	£		£
Capital	10,000	Purchases	3,000
Sales	4,000	Rent	500
Receivables	5,000	Payables	1,500
	19,000		19,000

Step 3 On side with smaller total insert figure which makes it add up to total and call this the balance carried down (balance c/d).

Cash account

	£		£
Capital	10,000	Purchases	3,000
Sales	4,000	Rent	500
Receivables	5,000	Payables	1,500
		Balance c/d	14,000
	19,000		19,000

Step 4 On the opposite side of the account enter this same figure below the total line and call it the balance brought down (balance b/d).

Cash account

	£		£
Capital	10,000	Purchases	3,000
Sales	4,000	Rent	500
Receivables	5,000	Payables	1,500
		Balance c/d	14,000
	19,000		19,000
Balance b/d	14,000		

This shows that after all of these transactions there is £14,000 of cash left as an asset in the business (a debit balance = an asset).

Preparing a trial balance

What is a trial balance?

- list of all of the ledger balances in the general ledger
- debit balances and credit balances are listed separately
- debit balance total should equal credit balance total.

Example

Simple trial balance

	Debit £	Credit £
Sales		5,000
Wages	100	
Purchases	3,000	
Rent	200	
Vehicle	3,000	
Receivables	100	
Payables		1,400
	6,400	6,400

Debit or credit balance?

If you are just given a list of balances you must know whether they are debit or credit balances.

Remember the rules!

Debit Balances	Credit Balances
Assets	Liabilities
Expenses	Income

Sales and purchases returns

Sales returns = debit balance
(opposite to sales)

Purchases returns = credit balance (opposite
to purchases)

Discounts allowed and discounts received

Discounts allowed = debit balance (expense)

Discounts received = credit balance (opposite
of an expense)

CBA focus

Returns and discounts are not as obvious as
other accounts as to whether they are debit
or credit balances so make sure that you
understand the logic behind these balances.

2

Accounting for VAT and payroll

- What is VAT?
- Rates of VAT.
- Calculation of VAT.
- Accounting for VAT.
- Payroll.

What is VAT?

- tax on consumer expenditure
- collected by HM Revenue and Customs (HMRC) as goods are bought and sold during the supply chain
- VAT-registered business charges VAT on sales (output tax) and incurs VAT on purchases (input tax)
- difference between the output tax and the input tax is the amount due to or from HMRC.

Rates of VAT

- different rates of VAT apply to different types of supplies.

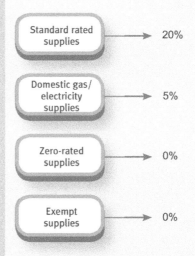

Standard rated supplies	→	20%
Domestic gas/ electricity supplies	→	5%
Zero-rated supplies	→	0%
Exempt supplies	→	0%

Zero-rated v Exempt

Zero rated	0%	If zero-rated goods are sold, VAT on purchases can still be recovered
Exempt	0%	If exempt supplies are sold, no VAT can be recovered on purchases – VAT becomes additional cost of business

Calculation of VAT

Example

Goods are sold for £1,000 exclusive (net) of VAT:

VAT $= £1,000 \times 20\% = £200$

Total value $= £1,000 + £200 = £1,200$

Goods are purchased for £600 inclusive of VAT (gross):

VAT $= £600 \times 20/120 = £100$

Net value $= £600 - £100 = £500$

Example

Goods are sold for £2,000 exclusive (net) of VAT:

VAT $= £2,000 \times 20\% = £400$

Total value $= £2,000 + £400 = £2,400$

Goods are purchased for £900 inclusive of VAT (gross):

VAT $= £900 \times 20/120 = £150$

Net value $= £900 - £150 = £750$

CBA focus

In the assessment you often have to calculate VAT on both sales/purchases which are exclusive (net) of VAT and sales/purchases which are inclusive of VAT (gross).

Accounting for VAT

- VAT on sales and purchases are normally recorded in the sales day book and purchases day book

- postings made from these books of prime entry to the ledger accounts

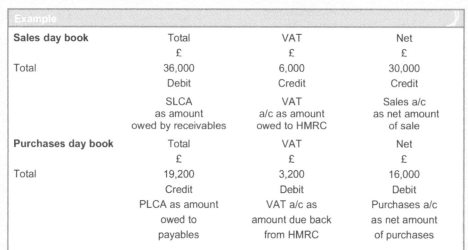

Example			
Sales day book	Total	VAT	Net
	£	£	£
Total	36,000	6,000	30,000
	Debit	Credit	Credit
	SLCA as amount owed by receivables	VAT a/c as amount owed to HMRC	Sales a/c as net amount of sale
Purchases day book	Total	VAT	Net
	£	£	£
Total	19,200	3,200	16,000
	Credit	Debit	Debit
	PLCA as amount owed to payables	VAT a/c as amount due back from HMRC	Purchases a/c as net amount of purchases

Sales account

	£		£
		SLCA	30,000

Sales ledger control account

	£		£
Sales	36,000		

VAT control account

	£		£
PLCA	3,200	SLCA	6,000

Purchases account

	£		£
PLCA	16,000		

Purchases ledger control account

	£		£
		Purchases	19,200

When all of the transactions for a quarter have been recorded, the VAT control account can be balanced to determine the amount due to or from HMRC.

VAT control account

	£		£
PLCA	3,200	SLCA	6,000
Balance c/d	2,800		
	6,000		6,000
		Balance b/d	2,800

This means that £2,800 is due to be paid to HMRC as it is a credit balance (liability).

This amount will have to be paid to HMRC – double entry:

Debit	VAT control account	£2,800
Credit	Bank account	£2,800

Debit balance on VAT account

If the balance b/d was a debit balance (asset), this would mean that the amount was due back from HMRC. When this VAT refund is received from HMRC, the double entry is:

Debit   Bank account

Credit   VAT control account

CBA focus

In the assessment you might be required to post the day books including the VAT.

You might also have to deal with errors that involve VAT so you need to understand the double entry.

Accounting for VAT

- sales shown net of VAT in SPL
- if VAT is recoverable, purchases/expenses shown net of VAT in SPL
- if VAT is irrecoverable, VAT is included in purchases/expenses in SPL
- VAT due to/from HMRC shown in statement of financial position as liability/asset.

Payroll

Overview of the payroll function

The responsibilities of payroll staff within an organisation include:

- calculating correctly the amount of pay due to each employee,
- ensuring each employee is paid on time with the correct amount,
- ensuring amounts due to external parties such as HM Revenue and Customs are correctly determined and paid on time.

Gross pay

Gross pay is the wage or salary due to the employee for the amount of work done in the period.

Net pay

Net pay is the amount that the employee will actually receive after appropriate deductions have been made.

PAYE

The PAYE scheme is a national scheme whereby employers withhold tax and other deductions from their employees' wages and salaries when they are paid. The deductions are then paid over monthly to HM Revenue and Customs by the employer.

National insurance

National Insurance is a state scheme run by HM Revenue and Customs which pays certain benefits including; retirement pensions, widow's allowances and pensions, jobseeker's allowance, incapacity benefit and maternity allowance. The scheme is funded by people who are currently in employment and have earnings above a certain level.

Accounting entries for wages and salaries

Payroll transactions are recorded by journal entries which traces the accounting entry from the payroll record to the journal book to being entered into the general ledger.

The accounting entries for wages and salaries are as follows:

---

1. Dr Wages expense account

Cr Wages and salaries control account

with the total expenses relating to the business (gross pay plus employer's NIC)

---

2. Dr Wages and salaries control account

Cr Bank account

with the net wages paid to the employees

---

3. Dr Wages and salaries control account

Cr HMRC liability

with those deductions made from the employees which are payable to the HM Revenue and Customs

---

If applicable it may also be necessary to record a payable to the pension fund and any other voluntary deductions that are made.

---

4. Dr Wages and salaries control account

Cr Pension / Other voluntary deduction liability

with those deductions made from the employees which are payable to the pension fund or other voluntary deduction.

3

Capital and revenue expenditure

- IAS 16 Property, plant and equipment.
- Capital and revenue expenditure.
- Financing purchases of non-current assets.
- Recording the purchase of non-current assets.
- Tangible and intangible non-current assets.

IAS 16 Property, plant and equipment

- covers accounting treatment of tangible non-current assets and depreciation.

Non-current assets = Long-term assets of the business

Tangible non-current assets = Long-term assets with physical form

Capital and revenue expenditure

Capital expenditure	Revenue expenditure

- expenditure to acquire/enhance economic benefits of non-current assets
- recorded in statement of financial position

- all other expenditure
- charged to statement of profit or loss

Accounting for capital expenditure

Initial purchase:

Debit   Non-current asset account

Credit   Bank account/payables account with cost of non-current asset

Financing purchases of non-current assets

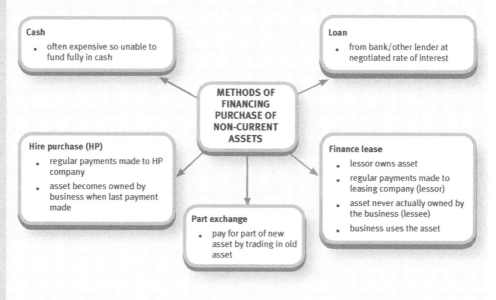

Cash
- often expensive so unable to fund fully in cash

Loan
- from bank/other lender at negotiated rate of interest

METHODS OF FINANCING PURCHASE OF NON-CURRENT ASSETS

Hire purchase (HP)
- regular payments made to HP company
- asset becomes owned by business when last payment made

Finance lease
- lessor owns asset
- regular payments made to leasing company (lessor)
- asset never actually owned by the business (lessee)
- business uses the asset

Part exchange
- pay for part of new asset by trading in old asset

Recording the purchase of non-current assets

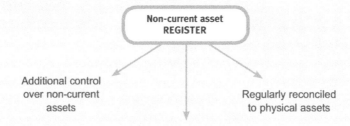

Typical layout

Non-current asset register – motor vehicles

Description/ serial number	Date acquired	Cost	Depreciation	Carrying amount	Funding method	Disposal proceeds	Disposal date
		£	£	£		£	
Ford Mondeo							
GN02 HGG	01/03/X2	16,000			Part-ex		
Y/e 31/12/X2			3,200	12,800			
Y/e 31/12/X3			2,560	10,240			
Honda Accord							
GN03 JFD	01/01/X3	18,000			Cash		
Y/e 31/12/X3			3,600	14,400			

- when an asset is purchased, as well as being recorded in the ledger account, it will also be recorded in the non-current asset register.

Tangible and intangible non-current assets

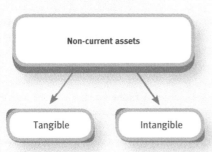

Non-current assets

Tangible

- physical form e.g. plant and machinery
- included in statement of financial position

Intangible

- no physical form e.g. goodwill
- often not included in statement of financial position

4

Depreciation

- What is depreciation?
- Calculating the depreciation charge.
- Accounting for depreciation charge.
- Calculating and recording depreciation charge.

What is depreciation?

Definition of depreciation

- measure of the cost of the economic benefits of non-current assets that have been consumed during the period
- consumption includes wearing out, using up or other reduction in the useful economic life of the non-current asset whether arising from use, effluxion of time or obsolescence.

Aim of depreciation

- for the expenditure on a non-current asset to be matched against the income generated by the asset throughout its useful economic life to the business.

Accounting concept relating to depreciation

- accruals concept

It is important that you realise that the purpose of depreciation is in accordance with the accruals concept and to spread the cost of the asset over the period in which it is being used within the business.

Calculating the depreciation charge

Three methods for AVBK

Straight line   Units of Production   Diminishing (reducing) balance

Straight line method

$$\text{Annual depreciation charge} = \frac{(\text{Cost} - \text{residual value})}{\text{Useful economic life}}$$

OR

$(\text{Cost} - \text{residual value}) \times \%$

This is a fixed percentage applied.

Definition

Residual value

- current estimate of sale/scrap value at the end of the useful life.

Useful economic life

- period over which the business will derive economic benefit from the asset.

e.g

Example

Machine purchased for £20,000 on 1 January 20X4. Expected to be used for 5 years with an anticipated scrap value at the end of that period of £6,500.

Solution

$$\text{Annual charge} = \frac{(\pounds20,000 - 6,500)}{5 \text{ years}}$$

$$= \pounds2,700$$

- same charge in each year of the asset's life.

Diminishing balance method

- fixed percentage applied to carrying amount
- carrying amount = cost less accumulated depreciation.

Example

Machine purchased for £20,000 on 1 January 20X4. Depreciation is at 20% per annum on the diminishing balance basis.

Solution

Charge for 20X4 = £20,000 x 20%
= £4,000

Charge for 20X5 = (£20,000 – £4,000)
x 20%
= £3,200

Charge for
20X6 = (£20,000 - £4,000 - £3,200)
x 20%

= £2,560

- depreciation charge is higher in early years of asset's life and lower in later years
- particularly suits assets such as motor vehicles for which higher benefits are consumed in the earlier years with reducing benefits as the years of use pass by.

Units of production method

- Based on the actual usage of the asset
- Higher depreciation is charged with higher usage
- Time is not important, activity level is.

Example

A machine has a cost of £10,000.	**Solution** Year 1 depreciation
It is depreciated based on the units of production. The asset has an estimated useful life of 10,000 units of production.	$£10,000 \times \dfrac{1,000}{10,000} = £1,000$
In year 1, 1,000 units were produced. In year 2, 1,500 units were produced. Show the amount of depreciation charged for years 1 and 2 of the machine's life.	Year 2 depreciation $£10,000 \times \dfrac{1,500}{10,000} = £1,500$

Accounting for depreciation charge

> **Depreciation charge – two effects:**

Expense in the statement of profit or loss

Reduction in value of asset in statement of financial position

Double entry:

Debit   Depreciation charge account

Credit   Accumulated depreciation account

Example

Machine purchased for £20,000 on 1 January 20X4. Expected to be used for 5 years with an anticipated scrap value at the end of that period of £6,500.

Straight line depreciation is to be used.

Solution

Step 1

Calculate annual depreciation charge:

$$\text{Annual charge} = \frac{(£20,000 - 6,500)}{5 \text{ years}}$$

$$= £2,700$$

Step 2

Open up depreciation charge account and accumulated depreciation account.

Depreciation charge account

£	£

Accumulated depreciation account

£	£

Step 3

Put through the double entry for 20X4:

Debit	Depreciation charge account	£2,700
Credit	Accumulated depreciation account	£2,700

Depreciation charge account

	£		£
Accumulated depreciation	2,700		

Accumulated depreciation account

	£		£
		Depreciation charge	2,700

Step 4

Balance the accounts:

- depreciation charge is transferred to the statement of profit or loss as an expense
- accumulated depreciation balance is shown on statement of financial position.

Depreciation charge account

	£		£
Accumulated depreciation	2,700	SPL	2,700
	2,700		2,700

Accumulated depreciation account

	£		£
Balance c/d	2,700	Depreciation charge	2,700
	2,700		2,700
		Balance b/d	2,700

Step 5

Produce statement of financial position entries:

Statement of financial position 31 December 20X4

	Cost £	Accum Dep'n £	£
Plant and machinery	20,000	(2,700)	17,300

Step 6

Repeat for following year, 20X5:

Depreciation charge account

	£		£
Accumulated depreciation	2,700	SPL	2,700
	2,700		2,700

Accumulated depreciation account

	£		£
		Balance b/d*	2,700
Balance c/d	5,400	Depreciation charge	2,700
	5,400		5,400
		Balance b/d	5,400

* Note that the balance from 20X4 is brought down.

Statement of financial position 31 December 20X5

	Cost £	Dep'n £	£
Plant and machinery	20,000	(5,400)	14,600

CBA focus

Accounting for non-current assets and depreciation is a large part of the examination and you will have to calculate depreciation charges and update account balances for depreciation using either the straight line, diminishing balance or units of production method.

Calculating and recording depreciation charge

- each year the depreciation charge is calculated for each asset and recorded in the non-current asset register
- then also recorded in the ledger accounts.

Example

Year ended 31/12/X4

Non-current asset register – motor vehicles

Description/ serial number	Date acquired	Cost £	Depreciation £	Carrying amount £	Funding method	Disposal proceeds £	Disposal date
Ford Mondeo							
GN02 HGG	01/03/X2	16,000			Part-ex		
Y/e 31/12/X2			3,200	12,800			
Y/e 31/12/X3			2,560	10,240			
Y/e 31/12/X4			**2,048**	**8,192**			
Honda Accord							
GN03 JFD	01/01/X3	18,000			Cash		
Y/e 31/12/X3			3,600	14,400			
Y/e 31/12/X4			**2,880**	**11,520**			

CBA focus

In the assessment you will be expected to complete a non-current asset register.

5

Disposal of capital assets

- Accounting for disposals.
- Part-exchange.
- Recording the disposal of non-current assets.
- Reconciling the non-current asset register to the physical assets.

Accounting for disposals

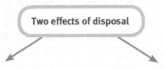

Two effects of disposal

Asset must be removed from statement of financial position
- remove asset at cost
- remove accumulated depreciation

Account for gain or loss on disposal recognised in the statement of profit or loss
- difference between proceeds and carrying amount

Entries made in disposal account

Example

A machine which cost £20,000 is sold for £10,000. Depreciation charge to date on the asset (balance on accumulated depreciation account) is £8,100.

Solution

Step 1

Transfer cost of asset from non-current asset account to disposal account.

Non-current asset account

	£		£
Balance b/d	20,000	Disposal account	20,000

Disposal account

	£		£
Non-current asset - cost	20,000		

Example

Step 2

Transfer accumulated depreciation to disposal account.

Accumulated depreciation account

	£		£
Disposal account	8,100	Balance b/d	8,100

Disposal account

	£		£
Non-current asset – cost	20,000	Accumulated dep'n	8,100

Step 3

Enter disposal proceeds in disposal account

Disposal account

	£		£
Non-current asset – cost	20,000	Accumulated dep'n	8,100
		Bank	10,000

Step 4

Balance disposal account to find gain or loss on disposal and transfer this to the statement of profit or loss.

Disposal account

	£		£
Non-current asset – cost	20,000	Accumulated dep'n	8,100
		Bank	10,000
		Loss on disposal SPL	1,900
	20,000		20,000

Loss on disposal can be checked:

	£
Cost of asset	20,000
Accumulated depreciation	(8,100)
Carrying amount	11,900
Disposal proceeds	(10,000)
Loss on disposal	1,900

Part-exchange

| Business | Dealer |

Business

Wants to acquire new asset.

Offers old asset in part-exchange.

Pays for remaining cost of new asset.

Part-exchange allowance/value

- effectively proceeds of old asset disposal.
- also part of cost of new asset.

Dealer

Agrees to take old asset in part-exchange.

Values old asset and gives part-exchange allowance.

Example

A business has a car which cost £15,000 and has accumulated depreciation to date of £10,000. A new car is to be acquired at a total cost of £18,000 but the car dealer will take the old car in part exchange and give a part-exchange allowance of £3,500.

Solution

Step 1

Transfer cost and accumulated depreciation to the disposal account.

Non-current asset at cost – old car

	£		£
Balance b/d	15,000	Disposal account	15,000

Accumulated depreciation – old car

	£		£
Disposal account	10,000	Balance b/d	10,000

Disposal account

	£		£
Non-current asset cost	15,000	Accumulated Depreciation	10,000

Step 2

Account for purchase of new car – payment is made for the difference between the total cost of £18,000 and the part-exchange allowance of £3,500 – i.e. £14,500.

Non-current asset at cost – new car

	£		£
Bank	14,500		

Example

Step 3

Account for part-exchange allowance:

- in disposal account treat as proceeds
- in non-current asset account treat as part of cost.

Debit Non-current asset at cost £3,500

Credit Disposal account £3,500

Disposal account

	£		£
Cost	15,000	Depreciation	10,000
		Non-current asset at cost	3,500

Non-current asset at cost – new car

	£		£
Bank	14,500		
Disposal – part exchange	3,500		

The non-current asset at cost account now shows the full cost of the new car of £18,000.

Step 4

Balance disposal account to find gain/loss on disposal.

Disposal account

	£		£
Cost	15,000	Depreciation	10,000
		Non-current asset at cost	3,500
		Loss on disposal	1,500
	15,000		15,000

CBA focus

In the assessment there may be a disposal of a non-current asset which must be accounted for. In most cases it will have a part-exchange involved as well so you must understand the accounting for this.

Recording the disposal of non-current assets

Example

Year ended 31/12/X5

On 30 June 20X5 the Ford Mondeo is sold for £7,000. The policy is to charge no depreciation in the year of disposal of an asset.

The details must be recorded in the non-current asset register.

Non-current asset register – motor vehicles

Description/ serial number	Date acquired	Cost £	Depreciation £	Carrying amount £	Funding method	Disposal proceeds £	Disposal date
Ford Mondeo							
GN02 HGG	01/03/X2	16,000			Part-ex		
Y/e 31/12/X2			3,200	12,800			
Y/e 31/12/X3			2,560	10,240			
y/e 31/12/X4			2,048	8,192			
y/e 31/12/X5						7,000	(30/6/X5)

Description/ serial number	Date acquired	Cost £	Depreciation £	Carrying amount £	Funding method	Disposal proceeds £	Disposal date
Honda Accord							
GN03 JFD	01/01/X3	18,000			Cash		
Y/e 31/12/X3			3,600	14,400			
Y/e 31/12/X4			2,880	11,520			
Y/e 31/12/X5			**2,304**	**9,216**			

Reconciling the non-current asset register to the physical assets

- purpose of non-current asset register is control of assets
- on a regular basis the assets recorded in the register must be checked to the physical assets held by the business
- discrepancies must be investigated.

DISCREPANCY

Asset in register but not physically present

- may have been sold but not recorded
- may be in another location
- may have been stolen

Asset on premises but not in register

- register may not be up-to-date
- asset may have been moved from another location

Reconciliation to ledger accounts

- the non-current asset register should also be agreed to the ledger account balances
- the non-current assets at cost ledger account balance should agree to the cost less disposals in the non-current asset register
- the accumulated depreciation ledger account balance should agree to the total of depreciation charges to date in the non-current asset register
- the total gain/loss in disposal column should agree to the amount credited/ charged to statement of profit or loss.

Extended trial balance
– an introduction

- Purpose of an extended trial balance.
- Layout of an extended trial balance.

Purpose of an extended trial balance

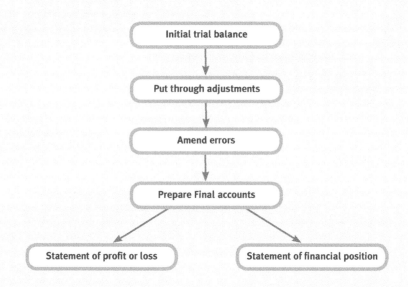

Layout of an extended trial balance

Typical ETB:

Account name	Trial balance		Adjustments		Statement of profit or loss		Statement of financial position	
	DR	CR	DR	CR	DR	CR	DR	CR
	£	£	£	£	£	£	£	£

7

Financial statements and ethical principles

- What are financial statements?
- Ethical principles.

What are financial statements?

Statement of profit or loss

- historic picture of all transactions
- during accounting period
- shows performance of business
- revenue and costs and final profit

Statement of financial position

- picture of the business on last day of accounting period
- shows position of business
- assets, liabilities, capital

Example

Statement of Profit or Loss for the year ended

	£	£	
Sales		X	
Opening Inventories	X		Known as trading account
Purchases	X		
	X		
Less: closing inventories	X		
Cost of sales		(X)	
Gross profit		X	
Less: expenses			
Rent and rates	X		
Heat and light	X		Known as Statement of Profit or Loss
Wages, etc	X		
		(X)	
Profit/loss for the year/period		X	

Example

Statement of financial position as at 30 September 20X7

Non-current assets	Cost £	Depreciation £	Carrying amount £
Machinery at cost	X	X	X
Current assets			
Inventory		X	
Receivables	X		
Less: allowance	X		
		X	
Prepayments		X	
Bank		X	
		X	

Current liabilities			
Payables	X		
Accruals	X		
		X	
Net current assets			X
Net assets			X
Capital			
Opening capital			X
Profit for the year			X
Less: drawings			X
			X

Alternative presentation format for the statement of financial position:

Example

Statement of financial position as at 30 September 20X7

Non-current assets	£ Cost	£ Depreciation	£ Carrying amount
Machinery at cost	X	X	X
Current assets			
Inventory		X	
Receivables	X		
Less: allowance	X		
		X	
Prepayments		X	
Bank		X	
			X
Total assets			X

Capital and liabilities:		£
Opening capital		X
Profit for the year		X
Less: drawings		X
		X
Current liabilities:		
Payables	X	
Accruals	X	
		X
		X

Note that the two formats of the statement of financial position show exactly the same information. In the first format, liabilities have been deducted from assets to arrive at net assets which is equal to proprietor's capital.

In the alternative format, non-current and current assets are totalled to show total assets. This is equal to proprietor's capital plus liabilities.

CBA focus

In the assessment you will be expected to complete an extended trial balance. You will be expected to know the figures that will appear in each of the statements. It is not a requirement of Advanced Bookkeeping to prepare the Statement of Profit or Loss or the Statement of Financial Position.

Ethical principles

Ethics can be defined as the "moral principles that govern a person's behaviour or the conducting of an activity".

The Code of Ethics for Professional Accountants, published by The International Federation of Accountants (IFAC), forms the basis for the ethical codes of many accountancy bodies.

Five key principles

Integrity

Integrity means that a member must be straightforward and honest in all professional and business relationships. Integrity also implies fair dealing and truthfulness.

Objectivity

Objectivity means that a member must not allow bias, conflict of interest or undue influence of others to override professional or business judgements.

Professional competence and due care

Professional competence means that a member has a continuing duty to maintain professional knowledge and skill at the level required to ensure that a client or employer receives competent professional service based on current developments in practice, legislation and techniques.

Due care means a member must act diligently and in accordance with applicable technical and professional standards when providing professional services.

Confidentiality

A member must, in accordance with the law, respect the confidentiality of information acquired as a result of professional and business relationships and not disclose any such information to third parties without proper and specific authority unless there is a legal or professional right or duty to disclose.

Confidential information acquired as a result of professional and business relationships must not be used for the personal advantage of the member or third parties.

Professional behaviour

A professional accountant should comply with relevant laws and regulations and should avoid any action that discredits the profession.

The importance of transparency and fairness

Transparency means openness (say, of discussions), clarity, lack of withholding of relevant information unless necessary.

Fairness means a sense of even-handedness and equality. Acting fairly is an ability to reach an equitable judgement in a given ethical situation.

8

Accounting for inventory

- Accounting for opening and closing inventory.
- Closing inventory reconciliation.
- Valuation of closing inventory.

Accounting for opening and closing inventory

At the beginning of the year

Figure for inventory is always opening inventory

Purchases during year

Always DEBIT purchases

Never make an entry in inventory account

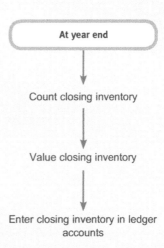

At year end

Count closing inventory

Value closing inventory

Enter closing inventory in ledger accounts

Trial balance

The trial balance will have a debit balance for opening inventory which is last year's closing inventory figure.

Inventory account

	£		£
Opening inventory	1,000		

Purchases during the year

Purchases during the year were £20,000.

Double entry:

Debit	Purchases account	£20,000
Credit	Bank/payables ledger control account	£20,000

No entry to the inventory account.

Year-end opening inventory and purchases

At end of the year, opening inventory account balance and purchases are cleared out to the statement of profit or loss:

Inventory account

	£		£
Opening inventory	1,000	Statement of profit or loss	1,000

Statement of profit or loss

	£	£
Sales (assumed figure)		35,000
Cost of sales		
Opening inventory	1,000	
Purchases	20,000	
	21,000	

Year-end closing inventory

Closing inventory at the year-end is valued at £2,000.

Enter closing inventory in inventory account

Double entry

Debit	Inventory account – Statement of financial position (asset) £2,000
Credit	Closing inventory – Statement of profit or loss £2,000

Inventory account

	£		£
Opening inventory	1,000	Statement of profit or loss	1,000

Closing Inventory – SFP

	£		£
Closing inventory SPL	2,000		

Closing Inventory SPL

			£
Statement of profit or loss	2,000	Closing inventory SFP	2,000

Statement of profit or loss

	£	£
Sales/Revenue		35,000
Cost of sales		
Opening inventory	1,000	
Purchases	20,000	
	21,000	
Less: closing inventory	(2,000)	
Cost of sales		(19,000)
Gross profit		16,000

Balance on closing inventory account remains in account as opening inventory for the following year.

Inventory account

	£		£
Balance b/d	2,000		

CBA focus

Carrying forward closing inventory rather than charging against profit for the year is an example of the accruals/matching concept. When the inventory is sold in the following year, it will form part of cost of sales as the opening inventory. So the cost is matched with the revenue earned from selling the inventory.

Closing inventory reconciliation

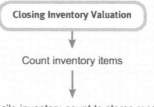

Closing Inventory Valuation

↓

Count inventory items

↓

Reconcile inventory count to stores records

↓

Value inventory

Stores records

- each line of inventory will have a bin card/inventory card
- shows quantity received from suppliers, issued for production/sale, returned to stores
- also shows quantity that should be on hand.

Reconciliation

 >

| Quantity counted | > | Bin card balance |

Possible reasons

- stores records not updated for delivery
- errors in stores records/counting.

 <

| Quantity counted | < | Bin card balance |

Possible reasons

- stores records not updated for sale/ return to supplier
- errors in stores records/counting
- items stolen.

Valuation of closing inventory

Inventory Valuation is the lower of

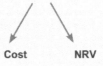

Cost   NRV

- lower of cost and net realisable value
- rule applies to each individual line of inventory.

Cost = expenditure incurred in normal course of business in bringing product to present location and condition.

= • purchase price
  • import duties
  • transport/handling costs
  • direct production costs
  • other overheads attributable to
  • bringing product to present location and condition.

Net realisable value = sales proceeds expected from future sale after deducting any further costs to completion and selling costs.

Example

Closing inventory has been valued at £13,500; included in this are items which originally cost £2,000 but due to damage can only be sold for £1,500.

Solution

	£
Cost	2,000
NRV	(1,500)
Inventory adjustment required	500

Journal:

Debit Closing inventory – SPL	£500
Credit Closing inventory – SFP	£500

Final value for closing inventory in SPL and SFP = £13,500 – £500 = £13,000

In most examinations you will be required to put through an adjustment such as this for the closing inventory valuation.

Valuation of inventory at the lower of cost and NRV is an example of prudence in accounting. If it is likely that a loss will be made on the sale of the items (i.e. NRV < cost) then this should be recognised immediately by writing down the inventory at cost to NRV.

9

Irrecoverable and doubtful debts

- Irrecoverable and doubtful debts.
- Accounting for irrecoverable debts.
- Accounting for doubtful debts.
- Types of allowance for doubtful debts.
- Recovery of debts.

Irrecoverable and doubtful debts

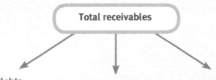

Total receivables

Irrecoverable debts (Bad debts)
- debts highly unlikely to be received
- written off

Doubtful debts
- debts which may not be received
- allowance made and shown in statement of financial position

Good debts
- debts which are highly likely to be received
- shown as current asset in statement of financial position

Accounting for irrecoverable debts

- as irrecoverable debt is highly unlikely to be received it is written out of the books
- therefore removed from receivables (SLCA).

Double entry

Debit   Irrecoverable debts expense account (SPL)

Credit Sales ledger control account (SFP)

Example

Business has total receivables of £10,000 but one customer owing £600 has gone into liquidation and it is unlikely any money will be received.

Solution

Sales ledger control account

	£		£
Balance b/d	10,000	Irrecoverable debts expense	600
		Balance c/d	9,400
	10,000		10,000
Balance b/d	9,400		

Irrecoverable debts expense account

	£		£
Sales ledger control account	600	Statement of profit or loss	600
	600		600

Statement of financial position – receivables appear as £9,400.

Statement of profit or loss – expense for irrecoverable debts of £600.

Accounting for doubtful debts

- doubtful debt not as clear-cut as irrecoverable debt
- might be received but might not
- it is prudent to reflect this in final accounts.

HOW?

Allowance for doubtful debts set up

Netted off against receivables in statement of financial position

Double entry

Debit   Allowance for doubtful debts adjustment (SPL)

Credit   Allowance for doubtful debts account (SFP)

Example

At end of first year of trading, a business has total receivables of £20,000 and it is decided that of this amount £1,000 is doubtful.

Solution

Sales ledger control account

	£		£
Balance b/d	20,000		

Allowance for doubtful debts account

	£		£
		Allowance for doubtful debt adjustment	1,000

Allowance for doubtful debt adjustment account

	£		£
Allowance for doubtful debts	1,000		

Statement of financial position – receivables shown as:

	£
Receivables	20,000
Less: allowance for doubtful debts	(1,000)
	19,000

Statement of profit or loss account – expense for £1,000 for setting up allowance.

Subsequent years

- once an allowance for doubtful debts account has been set up, it remains in the ledger accounts as a credit balance (statement of financial position item)

- each year adjusted for any increase/decrease required.

Year 2

At the end of year 2, receivables are £30,000 of which £1,200 are thought to be doubtful.

Solution

Step 1

Set up opening balance on allowance account (closing balance at end of previous year).

Allowance for doubtful debts account

	£		£
		Balance b/d	1,000

Step 2

Calculate allowance required at end of current year. In this example given as £1,200.

Step 3

Enter closing balance equal to the required new allowance. The figure to balance this account will be written off to the allowance for doubtful debt adjustment account.

Allowance for doubtful debts account

	£		£
Balance c/d	1,200	Balance b/d	1,000
		Allowance for doubtful debt adjustment account	200
	1,200		1,200
		Balance b/d	1,200

Allowance for doubtful debt adjustment account

	£		£
Allowance for doubtful debts	200		

Statement of financial position –
receivables shown as:

	£
Receivables	30,000
Less: allowance for doubtful debts	(1,200)
	28,800

Statement of profit or loss - expense for
£200 for increasing allowance.

Year 3

At end of year 3, receivables total £21,000
of which £900 are thought to be doubtful.

Solution

Step 1

Set up opening balance on allowance
account (closing balance at end of year 2).

Allowance for doubtful debts account

	£		£
		Balance b/d	1,200

Step 2

Calculate allowance required at end of
current year (in this example given as
£900).

Step 3

Enter closing balance equal to the required
new allowance (£900). The figure to
balance the account will be written off to
the Allowance for doubtful debt adjustment
account – in this case a write back to profit.

Allowance for doubtful debts account

	£		£
Allowance for doubtful debt adjustment account	300	Balance b/d	1,200
Balance c/d	900		
	1,200		1,200
		Balance b/d	900

Allowance for doubtful debt adjustment account

£		£
	Allowance for doubtful debts	300

Statement of financial position – receivables shown as:

	£
Receivables	21,000
Less: allowance for doubtful debts	(900)
	20,100

Statement of profit or loss – credited with £300 for decreasing allowance.

In the examination you will always have to deal with adjustments for irrecoverable debts and doubtful debts allowances. Remember that if there is already an allowance for doubtful debts then only the increase or decrease to the allowance needs to be charged/credited to the statement of profit or loss.

Types of allowance for doubtful debts

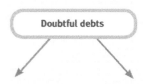

Doubtful debts

Specific allowance
- particular debt is identified as doubtful e.g. debt from Mr F

General allowance
- business experience indicates that a certain % of debts may not be paid e.g. 5%

Example

A business has a current allowance for doubtful debts of £500. Total receivables at the year-end are £31,000. It is decided to make an allowance for one particular debt of £800 and to make a general allowance against 2% of remaining receivables.

Solution

Step 1

Set up opening balance on allowance account.

Allowance for doubtful debts account

£		£
	Balance b/d	500

Step 2

Calculate allowance required at end of current year.

	£
Specific allowance	800
General allowance	
(£31,000 – £800) x 2%	604
Total allowance required	1,404

Step 3

Enter closing balance equal to the required new allowance (£1,404). The figure to balance the account will be written off to the allowance for doubtful debt adjustment account.

Allowance for doubtful debts account

	£		£
Balance c/d	1,404	Balance b/d	500
		Allowance for doubtful debt adjustment account	904
	1,404		1,404
		Balance b/d	1,404

Allowance for doubtful debt adjustment account

	£		£
Allowance for doubtful debts	904		

Statement of financial position – receivables shown as

	£
Receivables	31,000
Less: allowance for doubtful debts	1,404
	29,596

Statement of profit or loss – expense of £904 for increasing allowance.

Whether the allowance for doubtful debts is a specific or general provision or a mixture of the two, there is no difference in the basic accounting.

Calculate the allowance required at the year-end and enter this as the balance c/d on the account. The amount to balance the account will be written off/back to statement of profit or loss.

Recovery of debts

Debt previously written off

- debt is written off in one year
- in a later year it is unexpectedly received.

Double entry

Debit	Cash/bank account
Credit	Irrecoverable debts expense account

Debt previously provided for

- debt has allowance made against it in one year
- in a later year it is unexpectedly received
- debt is still in SLCA as it has not been written off.

Double entry

Debit	Cash/bank account
Credit	Sales ledger control account

10

Control account reconciliations

- Types of reconciliation.
- Sales ledger control account.
- Purchases ledger control account.
- Sales ledger control account reconciliation.
- Purchases ledger control account reconciliation.

Types of reconciliation

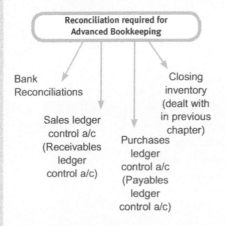

Reconciliation required for Advanced Bookkeeping

Bank Reconciliations

Sales ledger control a/c (Receivables ledger control a/c)

Purchases ledger control a/c (Payables ledger control a/c)

Closing inventory (dealt with in previous chapter)

Sales ledger control account

(also known as receivables ledger control account)

Typical sales ledger control account:

Sales ledger control account

	Note	£		Note	£
Balance b/d	(i)	3,400	SRDB	(iii)	1,800
SDB	(ii)	20,600	CRB – cash	(iv)	19.500
			Discounts allowed	(v)	1,200
			Irrecoverable debt write-off	(vi)	400
			Contra	(vii)	200
			Balance c/d		900
					24,000
		24,000			
Balance b/d		900			

Notes

(i) Opening balance = asset = debit balance

(ii) Sales invoices posted from sales day book

(iii) Credit notes posted from sales returns day book

(iv) Cash receipts posted from cash receipts book

(v) Discounts allowed posted from discounts allowed book

(vi) Irrecoverable debt written off (see earlier chapter)

(vii) Contra entry with purchases ledger control account.

Solution	
Double entry:	
Debit Purchases ledger control account	£200
Credit Sales ledger control account	£200

Purchases ledger control account (also known as payables ledger control account)

Typical purchases ledger control account:

Purchases ledger control account

	Note	£		Note	£
PRDB	(iii)	900	Balance b/d	(i)	2,100
CPB – cash	(iv)	13,300	PDB	(ii)	15,800
Discounts received	(v)	700			
Contra entry	(vi)	200			
Balance c/d		2,800			
		17,900			17,900
			Balance b/d		2,800

Example

Contra entry

- a customer who owes us £200 is also a supplier and we owe him £300. It has been agreed that the two amounts should be set off by a contra entry, leaving only £100 owed by us to the supplier.

Notes

(i) Opening balance = liability = credit balance

(ii) Purchases invoices posted from purchases day book

(iii) Credit notes posted from purchases returns day book

(iv) Cash paid to suppliers posted from cash payments book

(v) Discounts received posted from discounts received book

(vi) Contra entry (see above).

Sales ledger control account reconciliation

- the sales ledger control account is written up using totals from sales day book, sales returns day book, discounts allowed book and cash receipts book.
- individual accounts for receivables in the subsidiary (sales) ledger are written up using the individual entries from the sales day book, sales returns day book, discounts allowed book and cash receipts book.
- as both are written up from the same sources of information, at the end of the period the balance on the sales ledger control account should equal the total of the list of balances in the subsidiary (sales) ledger.

$$\boxed{\text{SLCA balance}} = \boxed{\begin{array}{c}\text{Total of list of}\\\text{subsidiary (sales)}\\\text{ledger balances}\end{array}}$$

Purpose of sales ledger control account reconciliation

- to show that the balance in the SLCA does in fact equal the total of the list of balances
- to indicate that there are errors in either the SLCA or the subsidiary (sales) ledger accounts if the two are not equal
- to find the correct figure for total receivables to appear in the trial balance.

Preparing a sales ledger control account reconciliation.

Step 1

- extract list of balances from the subsidiary (sales)

Step 2

- balance the sales ledger control account.

Step 3

- If the two figures are different, the reasons for the difference must be investigated.

Step 4

- correct any errors that affect the sales ledger control account
- find corrected balance on the sales ledger control account.

Step 5

- correct any errors that affect the total of the list of balances from the subsidiary (sales) ledger
- find corrected total of list of subsidiary (sales) ledger balances.

Example

Sales ledger control account reconciliation

The balance on the sales ledger control account at 31 May is £4,100. The individual balances on the subsidiary (sales) ledger are as follows:

	£
receivable A	1,200
receivable B	300
receivable C	2,000
receivable D	1,000

Step 1

Extract list of balances from the subsidiary (sales) ledger accounts and total.

	£
receivable A	1,200
receivable B	300
receivable C	2,000
receivable D	1,000
	4,500

Step 2

- Balance the sales ledger control account.

The balance has been given as £4,100.

Step 3

- If the two figures are different, the reasons for the difference must be investigated.

You are given the following information:

- a page of the sales day book had been undercast by £100
- a credit note for £50 to Receivable A had been entered into A's subsidiary (sales) ledger account as an invoice
- a contra entry with Receivable B for £200 had only been entered in the sales ledger control account not the individual subsidiary sales ledger account.

Step 4

- correct any errors that affect the sales ledger control account
- Find corrected balance on sales ledger control account.

Sales ledger control account			
	£		£
Original balance	4,100	Corrected balance	4,200
SDB undercast	100		
	4,200		4,200
Corrected balance	4,200		

If the sales day book was undercast, then the amount posted to the sales ledger control account was £100 too small and therefore an additional debit entry for £100 is needed in the control account.

The other two adjustments affect the individual accounts not the control account.

Step 5

- correct any errors that affect the total of the list of balances from the subsidiary (sales) ledger

- Find corrected total of list of sales ledger balances.

	£
Subsidiary (sales) ledger account	
list total	4,500
Less:	
Credit note entered as invoice	(100)
Less: Contra	(200)
Corrected list of balances	4,200

As the credit note for £50 had been entered as an invoice instead, the list of balances must be reduced by £100 to reflect the removal of the invoice and the entry of the credit note.

The contra had only been entered in the sales ledger control account and therefore the same £200 must be deducted from the list of balances.

Credit balances on sales ledger accounts

- normally a receivables balance on the subsidiary (sales) ledger account will be a debit balance brought down (asset balance – money owed from receivable)
- sometimes, however, the balance will be a credit balance.

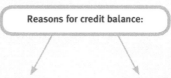

Reasons for credit balance:

Overpayment by receivable

Misposting to subsidiary (sales) ledger account

Treatment of credit balance

- when the list of sales ledger balances is drawn up and totalled, the credit balance must be deducted rather than added.

Purchases ledger control account reconciliation

- the purchases ledger control account is written up using totals from purchases day book, purchases returns day book, discounts received book and cash payments book
- individual accounts for payables in the subsidiary (purchases) ledger are written up using the individual entries from the purchases day book, purchases returns day book, discounts received book and cash payments book
- as both are written up from the same sources of information, then at the end of the period the balance on the purchases ledger control account should equal the total of the list of balances in the subsidiary (purchases) ledger.

$$\boxed{\text{PLCA balance}} = \boxed{\begin{array}{c}\text{Total of list} \\ \text{of subsidiary} \\ \text{(purchases)} \\ \text{ledger balances}\end{array}}$$

Purpose of purchases ledger control account reconciliation

- to show that PLCA does in fact equal the total of the list of balances
- to indicate that there are errors in either the PLCA or the subsidiary (purchases) ledger accounts if the two are not equal
- to find the correct figure for total payables to appear in the trial balance.

Preparing a purchases ledger control account reconciliation

Step 1

- extract list of balances from subsidiary (purchases) ledger accounts and total.

Step 2

- balance the purchases ledger control account.

Step 3

- if the two figures are different the reasons for the difference must be investigated.

Step 4

- correct any errors that affect the purchases ledger control account
- find corrected balance on purchases ledger control account.

Step 5

- correct any errors that affect the total of the list of balances from the subsidiary purchases ledger
- find corrected total of list of subsidiary purchases ledger balances.

Example

Purchases ledger control account reconciliation

The balance on the purchases ledger control account at 31 May is £2,000. The individual balances on the subsidiary (purchases) ledger are as follows:

	£
payable E	800
payable F	600
payable G	400
payable H	700

Step 1

- Extract list of balances from subsidiary (purchases) ledger accounts and total.

	£
payable E	800
payable F	600
payable G	400
payable H	700
	2,500

Step 2

- Balance the purchases ledger control account.

The balance has been given as £2,000.

Step 3

- If the two figures are different, the reasons for the difference must be investigated.

You are given the following information:

- a page of the purchases returns day book had been overcast by £1,000
- discounts received from suppliers totalling £680 had not been posted to the control account
- an invoice from payable G for £350 had been entered into the individual account in the purchases ledger as £530.

Step 4

- correct any errors that affect the purchases ledger control account
- find corrected balance on purchases ledger control account.

Purchase ledger control account

	£		£
Discounts received	680	Original balance	2,000
Corrected balance	2,320	PRDB overcast	1,000
	3,000		3,000
		Corrected balance	2,320

If the purchases returns day book was overcast, then the amount posted to the purchases ledger control account on the debit side for returns was £1,000 too big and therefore an additional credit entry for £1,000 is needed in the control account.

The discounts received of £680 were omitted from the control account and therefore the control account must be debited with this amount.

Step 5

- correct any errors that affect the total of the list of balances from the subsidiary (purchases) ledger

- find corrected total of list of balances.

	£
Subsidiary (purchases) ledger account list total	2,500
Less: 'transposition error' on invoice (530 – 350)	(180)
Corrected list of balances	2,320

The invoice had been entered as £180 higher than it should have been and therefore the total of the list of balances must reduced by £180.

Debit balances on purchases ledger accounts

- normally a payable's balance on his subsidiary (purchases) ledger account will be a credit balance brought down (liability – money owed to payable)

- sometimes, however, the balance will be a debit balance.

Reasons for debit balance:

Overpayment to payable

Misposting to subsidiary (purchases) ledger account

Treatment of debit balance

- when the list of subsidiary (purchases) ledger balances is drawn up and totalled, the debit balance must be deducted rather than added.

11

Bank reconciliations

- Bank control account reconciliation.

Bank control account reconciliation

At regular intervals the cashier must check that the cash book is correct by comparing the cash book with the bank statement.

Why might they not agree?

Cheques we've paid in have not yet been cleared = "uncleared lodgements"
(Bank statement not fully up to date – our records fine).

Cheques we have written have not yet been taken to bank by the recipients or have not yet cleared = "unpresented cheques"
(Bank statement not fully up to date – our records fine).

Bank Charges / Interest we haven't accounted for (need to update our records for these).

Example

The following differences have been identified when comparing the cash book with the bank statements.

(i) Bank interest received £80, had not been entered in the cashbook

(ii) A BACS receipt of £12,400 and £920 from two customers has not been entered in the cashbook

(iii) A receipt for £1,300 has been recorded in the cashbook as £1,500

(iv) Cheques drawn for £7,880 entered in the cashbook are not showing on the bank statement.

Using the table below show those items that would be required to update the cashbook.

Adjustment	Amount £	Debit	Credit
(i)	80	✓	
(ii)	13,320	✓	
(iii)	200		✓

12

Accruals and prepayments

- Accruals concept.
- Accrued expenses.
- Prepaid expenses.
- Accrued and prepaid income.

Accruals concept

```
Accruals concept
```

Income/expenses dealt with in statement of profit or loss in period in which earned/incurred not period in which cash received/paid

Accrued expenses

An accrued expense is an expense incurred but not yet paid for. In accordance with the accruals concept the expense and a corresponding liability should be recognised.

Example			
A business has a year end of 31 December. On 1 May 20X5 a new building was rented with quarterly rentals in arrears of £1,500.	Date	Quarter ended	£
	31 July	31 July X5	1,500
	31 Oct	31 Oct X5	1,500
Payments for the year ended 31 December 20X5 were:	What is the accrual for rent at 31 December 20X5?		

Solution

£3,000 is recorded in the rent account as an expense (the cash paid):

Rent expenses

	£		£
31 July X5 Bank	1,500		
31 Oct X5 Bank	1,500		

However, the building has been occupied during November and December even though the rent has not yet been paid. This must be accrued:

Accrual	=	£1,500 x 2/3
	=	£1,000

Accounting entry for accrued expense:

Dr Rent expenses (SPL)
Cr Accrued expenses (SFP)

The debit entry increases the expense recognised in the rent expenses account within the SPL.

The credit entry recognises a liability in the SFP.

Statement of – charge of £4,000 (8 months
profit or loss   @ £500 per month)

Statement of – accrual of £1,000 in
financial   current liabilities
position

Continuing the previous example, the business continues to rent the building during 20X6.

Payments of rent are as follows:

Date	Quarter ended	£
31 Jan	31 Jan X6	1,500
30 Apr	30 Apr X6	1,500
31 July	31 July X6	1,800
31 Oct	31 Oct X6	1,800

Write up the ledger account for year ended 31 December 20X6.

Solution

Step 1

Enter the reversal of the opening accrued expense as a credit balance (£1,500 x 2/3 months).

Rent expenses

	£		£
		1 Jan X6 Reversal of accrued expenses	1,000

Step 2

Enter payments for the year:

Rent expenses

		£		£
31 Jan X6 Bank		1,500	1 Jan X6	
30 Apr X6 Bank		1,500	Reversal	1,000
31 July X6 Bank		1,800	of accrued	
31 Oct X6 Bank		1,800	expenses	

Step 3

Calculate the closing accrual (November and December rent not yet paid):

Accrual = £1,800 x 2/3 months
        = £1,200

Step 4

Enter closing accrual in the rent account and balance the account to find the rent charge for the year to 31 December 20X6:

Rent account			
	£		£
31 Jan X6 Bank	1,500	1 Jan X6 Reversal of accrued expenses	1,000
30 Apr X6 Bank	1,500		
31 July X6 Bank	1,800	31 Dec X6	
31 Oct X6 Bank	1,800	Expense for the year	6,800
31 Dec X6 Accrued expenses	1,200		
			7,800
	7,800	1 Jan X7 Reversal of accrued expenses	1,200

Proof of SPL charge	£
Jan X6 to April X6 (4 months @ £500 per month)	2,000
May X6 to Dec X6 (8 months @ £600 per month)	4,800
Total rent expense	6,800

Prepaid expenses

A prepaid expense is an expense already paid for although it has not yet been incurred so that an asset should be recognised.

Example

1 April 20X5 insurance policy for £6,000 taken out payable for next 12-month period. Business has 31 December year-end. Write up the ledger account for the year to 31 December 20X5.

Solution

Year to 31 December 20X5:

Insurance account		
	£	£
1 Apr X5 Bank	6,000	

At 31 December 20X5 insurance has already been paid for January to March 20X6:

Prepayment = £6,000 x 3/12
= £1,500

Accounting entry for prepaid expense:

Dr Prepaid expenses (SFP)
Cr Insurance expenses (SPL)

The credit entry decreases the expense recognised in the insurance expenses account within the SPL as although it was paid for it does not relate to this accounting period.

The debit entry recognises an asset in the SFP.

Insurance account			
	£		£
1 Apr X5 Bank	6,000	31 Dec X5 Expense for year	4,500
		31 Dec X5 Prepaid expenses	1,500
	6,000		6,000

SPL charge = £4,500 (9 months' insurance @ £500 per month)

SFP = £1,500 prepayment (debit balance brought down on insurance account) shown in current assets

Continuing the example, the insurance payment on 1 April 20X6 increases to £8,400.

First the reversal of the opening prepaid expense as a debit balance must be made.

Solution

Insurance account

	£		£
1 Jan X6 Reversal of prepaid expenses	1,500	31 Dec X6 Expense for the year	7,800
1 Apr X6 Bank	8,400	31 Dec X6 Prepaid expenses (8,400x3/12)	2,100
	9,900		9,900
1 Jan X7 Reversal of prepaid expense	2,100		

Proof of SPL charge

	£
Jan X6 to March X6 – 3 months @ £500 per month	1,500
April X6 to December X6 – 9 months @ £700 per month	6,300
Total SPL charge	7,800

CBA focus

In the examination you will have to deal with accruals and prepayments in many different contexts such as adjusting a trial balance figure and putting adjustments onto an extended trial balance. However, in many examinations you will also be required to complete an expense account showing opening and closing accruals or prepayments and the statement of profit or loss charge for the period.

Opening accruals and prepayments are the reversal of the prior accounting period's closing accruals and prepayments.

Accrued and prepaid income

- e.g. rent received
- income credited to SPL is amount earned in period not cash received

Cash received > income earned = income prepaid

Cash received < income earned = income accrued

Example

Business has two properties which it rents out.

| Property A | Rental £8,000 per annum Cash received £10,000 |
| Property B | Rental £6,000 per annum Cash received £5,000 |

Solution

Rental income – property A

	£		£
Income for the year	8,000	Cash	10,000
Prepaid income	2,000		
	———		———
	10,000		10,000
	———		———
		Reversal of prepaid income	2,000

Rental income – property B

	£		£
Income for the year	6,000	Cash	5,000
		Accrued income	1,000
	———		———
	6,000		6,000
	———		———
Reversal of accrued income	1,000		

Statement of financial position

	£
Current asset	
Accrued income	1,000
Current liabilities	
Income prepaid	2,000

13

Suspense accounts and errors

- What is a trial balance?
- Errors.
- Journal entries.
- Suspense account.
- Correcting errors.
- Errors and the suspense account.
- Clearing the suspense account.

What is a trial balance?

- a list of all of the ledger balances in the general ledger
- debit and credit balances are listed separately
- debit balance total should equal credit balance total

Illustration – trial balance

	Debit balances £	Credit balances £
Sales		5,000
Wages	100	
Purchases	3,000	
Rent	200	
Car	3,000	
SLCA	100	
PLCA		1,400
	6,400	6,400

Errors

In a manual accounting system, errors will be made – some are identified by extracting a trial balance but others will not be.

Single entry
- only one side of an entry made

Casting error
- account incorrectly balanced

ERRORS IDENTIFIED BY EXTRACTING A TRIAL BALANCE

Transposition error
- numbers transposed in recording i.e. 98 shown as 89

Extraction error
- account balance entered on trial balance as wrong figure

Errors of original entry

- error made when transaction first entered into primary records

Compensating errors

- two or more errors which are exactly equal and opposite

ERRORS NOT IDENTIFIED BY EXTRACTING A TRIAL BALANCE

Errors of omission

- a transaction is not entered at all in the primary records

Errors of principle

- entry made in fundamentally wrong type of account i.e. revenue expense entered into capital/ non-current asset account

Errors of commission

- entry made in wrong account although account of the correct type i.e. rent expense entered into electricity expense account

Journal entries

- written instruction to bookkeeper to put through a double entry which has not come from books of prime entry
- also used for correction of errors/adjustments/unusual items
- only used for adjusting double entry errors in the general ledger – not used for entries in the subsidiary (sales) or subsidiary (purchases) ledgers.

Journal format				
Date	Narrative	Account ref	Debit	Credit
			£	£
1 May	Electricity	GL014	200	
	Advertising	GL022		200

Being correction of misposting of electricity bill to advertising account

Suspense account

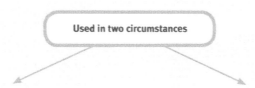

Used in two circumstances

Bookkeeper does not know what to do with one side of an entry and therefore posts it to a suspense account.

Example

£200 received but bookkeeper does not know what it is for so debits cash receipts book and credits suspense account.

When trial balance totals disagree used to balance the trial balance temporarily.

Example

Total of debit balances on trial balance is £35,000 but total of credit balances is £34,000. £1,000 credited to suspense account to make trial balance equal.

Correcting errors

- errors corrected by putting through a journal for the correcting entry.

How to find correcting entry

- work out the double entry that has been done
- work out the double entry that should have been done
- draft journal entry to go from what has been done to what should have been done.

Example

Journal entries

(i) An amount of £200 of electricity bill payments was entered into the advertising account.

What has been done?

| Debit | Advertising account | £200 |
| Credit | Bank account | £200 |

What should have been done?

| Debit | Electricity account | £200 |
| Credit | Bank account | £200 |

Journal entry

| Debit | Electricity account | £200 |
| Credit | Advertising account | £200 |

(ii) A purchase invoice for £1,000 had not been entered into the books of prime entry (ignore VAT).

What has been done?

No entries at all

What should have been done?

| Debit | Purchases account | £1,000 |
| Credit | PLCA | £1,000 |

Journal entry

Debit   Purchases account   £1,000

Credit   PLCA   £1,000

(iii) An irrecoverable debt for £100 is to be written off.

This is not correction of an error but an adjustment to be made.

Journal entry

Debit   irrecoverable debts
         expense account   £100

Credit   SLCA   £100

(iv) A contra entry for £500 has been entered in the general ledger control accounts but has not been entered in the subsidiary (purchases) ledger.

No journal entry is required as the error is not in the general ledger but the subsidiary ledger. However, the payables account in the subsidiary (purchases) ledger must be debited to reflect this contra entry.

CBA focus

In most examinations you will be required to draft journal entries to correct errors. However, you are normally told not to include any narrative so read the question carefully.

Errors and the suspense account

Some errors made will affect the trial balance and therefore are effectively part of the suspense account balance.

Example

(i) Discounts allowed of £150 have been entered as a credit entry in the discounts allowed account.

What has been done?

Credit Discounts allowed account	£150
Credit Sales ledger control account	£150

What should have been done?

Debit Discounts allowed account	£150
Credit Sales ledger control account	£150

Journal

Debit Discounts allowed account	£300
Credit Suspense account	£300

The discounts allowed account has been credited rather than debited with £150; therefore, to turn this into a debit of £150, it needs to be debited with £300. No other account is incorrect so the other side of the entry is to the suspense account.

(ii) The balance for motor expenses of £400 has been omitted from the trial balance.

What has been done?

The motor expenses balance of £400 has been omitted from the trial balance.

What should be done?

A £400 debit balance (expense) must appear on the trial balance.

Journal

Debit	Motor expenses (TB)	£400
Credit	Suspense account	£400

Clearing the suspense account

The suspense account cannot remain as a permanent account and must eventually be investigated and cleared.

Example

A business has a suspense account with a debit balance of £80.

The following errors were noted:

(i) rent of £750 was entered into the rent account as £570

(ii) an advertising bill was overstated in the advertising account by £100

Journals

(i) Debit   Rent account   £180
    Credit Suspense account   £180

(ii) Debit   Suspense account   £100
     Credit Advertising account   £100

Suspense account

	£		£
Opening balance	80	Rent	180
Advertising	100		
	180		180

The suspense account is now cleared.

CBA focus

In most examinations you will be required to draft journal entries to clear a suspense account balance or to put adjustments through an extended trial balance in order to clear the suspense account.

14

Extended trial balance
– in action

- Preparing an extended trial balance.

Preparing an extended trial balance

Step 1

Enter each ledger name and balance in trial balance columns.

Step 2

Total initial trial balance columns to ensure they are equal or set up a suspense account.

Step 3

Put through adjustments/amend errors in adjustments columns.

Step 4

Total adjustments columns to ensure double entry correct.

Step 5

Cross-cast each account line and enter total in either SPL or SFP columns.

Step 6

Total SPL a/c columns

– difference will be the profit/loss to be entered in SFP column as well.

Step 7

Total SFP columns.

Example

Initial trial balance of a sole trader at 30 June 20X6:

	£	£
Sales		40,000
Purchases	20,000	
Inventory at 1 July 20X5	2,000	
Non-current assets at cost	40,000	
Accumulated depreciation at 1 July 20X5		18,000
Sales ledger control account	4,400	
Bank	1,000	
Purchases ledger control		2,500
Drawings	10,000	
Capital		28,100
Rent	2,400	
Wages	5,600	
Heat and light	3,200	
	88,600	88,600

The following points are also noted:

(i) Depreciation charge at 15% straight line is to be provided for the year

(ii) There is an accrual for electricity of £300

(iii) There is a prepayment of rent of £500

(iv) An irrecoverable debt of £400 is to be written off

(v) An allowance of 5% of remaining receivables is to be set up for doubtful debts

(vi) Closing inventory has been valued at £2,200.

Solution

Step 1

Enter each ledger name and balance in trial balance columns.

Account name	Trial balance		Adjustments		Statement of profit or loss		Statement of financial position	
	DR	CR	DR	CR	DR	CR	DR	CR
	£	£	£	£	£	£	£	£
Sales		40,000						
Purchases	20,000							
Inventory at 1 July 20X5	2,000							
Non-current assets at cost	40,000							
Accumulated depreciation at 1 July 20X5		18,000						
Sales ledger control	4,400							
Bank	1,000							
Purchases ledger control		2,500						
Drawings	10,000							
Capital		28,100						
Rent	2,400							
Wages	5,600							
Heat and light	3,200							

Step 3

Put through adjustments/amend errors in adjustments columns

We will firstly draft journal entries for each adjustment then enter them into the ETB.

(i) Depreciation charge at 15% straight line is to be provided for the year

Depreciation charge = £40,000 x 15%

= £6,000

Journal

| Debit | Depreciation charge | £6,000 |
| Credit | Accumulated depreciation | £6,000 |

As there is no depreciation charge account, this must be set up when entered onto the ETB

(ii) There is an accrual for electricity of £300

Journal

| Debit | Heat and Light | £300 |
| Credit | Accruals | £300 |

Accruals account must be set up on ETB

(iii) There is a prepayment of rent of £500

Journal

| Debit | Prepayments | £500 |
| Credit | Rent | £500 |

Prepayments account must be set up on ETB

(iv) An irrecoverable debt of £400 is to be written off

Journal

Debit   Irrecoverable debts expense £400

Credit   Sales ledger control   £400

Irrecoverable expense account must be set up on ETB

(v) An allowance of 5% of remaining receivables is to be set up for doubtful debts

Amount of allowance = (£4,400 – £400) x 5%

= £200

Journal

Debit   Allowance for doubtful debt adjustment   £200

Credit   Allowance for doubtful debts £200

Allowance for doubtful debts account must be set up on ETB

(vi) Closing inventory has been valued at £2,200

Debit   Inventory account – SFP   £2,200

Credit inventory account – SPL   £2,200

Both of these accounts must be set up on the ETB.

Account name	Trial balance		Adjustments		Statement of profit or loss		Statement of financial position	
	DR £	CR £	DR £	CR £	DR £	CR £	DR £	CR £
Sales		40,000						
Purchases	20,000							
Inventory at 1 July 20X5	2,000							
Non-current assets at cost	40,000							
Accumulated depreciation at 1 July 20X5		18,000		6,000				
Sales ledger control	4,400			400				
Bank	1,000							
Purchases ledger control		2,500						
Drawings	10,000							
Capital		28,100						
Rent	2,400			500				
Wages	5,600							
Heat and light	3,200		300					
Depreciation charge			6,000					
Accruals				300				
Prepayments			500					
Irrecoverable debts expense			400					
Allowance for doubtful debt adjustment			200					
Allowance for doubtful debts				200				
Inventory – SFP			2,200					
Inventory – SPL				2,200				
	88,600	88,600						

Step 4: Total adjustments columns to ensure double entry correct. Make sure that you leave a spare line at the bottom for the net profit/loss figure in step 6.

Account name	Trial balance		Adjustments		Statement of profit or loss		Statement of financial position	
	DR £	CR £	DR £	CR £	DR £	CR £	DR £	CR £
Sales		40,000						
Purchases	20,000							
Inventory at 1 July 20X5	2,000							
Non-current assets at cost	40,000							
Accumulated depreciation at 1 July 20X5		18,000		6,000				
Sales ledger control	4,400			400				
Bank	1,000							
Purchases ledger control		2,500						
Drawings	10,000							
Capital		28,100						
Rent	2,400			500				
Wages	5,600							
Heat and light	3,200		300					
Depreciation charge			6,000					
Accruals				300				
Prepayments			500					
Irrecoverable debts expense			400					
Allowance for doubtful debt adjustment			200					
Allowance for doubtful debts				200				
Inventory – SFP			2,200					
Inventory – SPL				2,200				
	88,600	88,600	9,600	9,600				

Step 5

Cross-cast each account line and enter total in either SPL a/c or SFP column.

Income/expense accounts are entered in the SPL a/c columns.

Asset/liability accounts are entered in the SFP columns.

CBA focus

Take care with drawings as these are a statement of financial position item, being a reduction in capital.

Extended trial balance – in action

Account name	Trial balance		Adjustments		Statement of profit or loss		Statement of financial position	
	DR £	CR £	DR £	CR £	DR £	CR £	DR £	CR £
Sales		40,000				40,000		
Purchases	20,000				20,000			
Inventory at 1 July 20X5	2,000				2,000			
Non-current assets at cost	40,000						40,000	
Accumulated depreciation at 1 July 20X5		18,000		6,000				24,000
Sales ledger control	4,400			400			4,000	
Bank	1,000						1,000	
Purchases ledger control		2,500						2,500
Drawings	10,000						10,000	
Capital		28,100						28,100
Rent	2,400			500	1,900			
Wages	5,600				5,600			
Heat and light	3,200		300		3,500			
Depreciation charge			6,000		6,000			
Accruals				300				300
Prepayments			500				500	
Irrecoverable debts expense			400		400			
Allowance for doubtful debt adjustment			200		200			
Allowance for doubtful debts				200				200
Inventory – SFP			2,200				2,200	
Inventory – SPL				2,200	2,200			
	88,600	88,600	9,600	9,600				

Step 6

Total SPL a/c columns – the difference will be profit/loss to be entered in SFP column as well.

When the difference is found between the two IS column totals, this must be entered to make the two columns equal.

Debit entry = Profit = Credit entry in SFP

Credit entry = Loss = Debit entry in SFP

Step 7

Total SFP columns

Step 6

Account name	Trial balance		Adjustments		Statement of profit or loss		Statement of financial position	
	DR £	CR £	DR £	CR £	DR £	CR £	DR £	CR £
Sales		40,000				40,000		
Purchases	20,000				20,000			
Inventory at 1 July 20X5	2,000				2,000			
Non-current assets at cost	40,000						40,000	
Accumulated depreciation at 1 July 20X5		18,000		6,000				24,000
Sales ledger control	4,400			400			4,000	
Bank	1,000						1,000	
Purchases ledger control		2,500						2,500
Drawings	10,000						10,000	
Capital		28,100						28,100
Rent	2,400			500	1,900			
Wages	5,600				5,600			
Heat and light	3,200		300		3,500			
Depreciation charge			6,000		6,000			
Accruals				300				300
Prepayments			500				500	
Irrecoverable debts expense			400		400			
Allowance for doubtful debt adjustment			200		200			
Allowance for doubtful debts				200				200
Inventory – SFP			2,200				2,200	
Inventory – SPL				2,200		2,200		
Net profit					2,600			2,600
	88,600	88,600	9,600	9,600	42,200	42,200		

Step 7

Account name	Trial balance		Adjustments		Statement of profit or loss		Statement of financial position	
	DR £	CR £	DR £	CR £	DR £	CR £	DR £	CR £
Sales		40,000				40,000		
Purchases	20,000				20,000			
Inventory at 1 July 20X5	2,000				2,000			
Non-current assets at cost	40,000						40,000	
Accumulated depreciation at 1 July 20X5		18,000		6,000				24,000
Sales ledger control	4,400			400			4,000	
Bank	1,000						1,000	
Purchases ledger control		2,500						2,500
Drawings	10,000						10,000	
Capital		28,100						28,100
Rent	2,400			500	1,900			
Wages	5,600				5,600			
Heat and light	3,200		300		3,500			
Depreciation charge			6,000		6,000			
Accruals				300				300
Prepayments			500				500	
Irrecoverable debts expense			400		400			
Allowance for doubtful debt adjustment			200		200			
Allowance for doubtful debts				200				200
Inventory – SFP			2,200				2,200	
Inventory – SPL				2,200		2,200		
Net profit					2,600			2,600
	88,600	88,600	9,600	9,600	42,200	42,200	57,700	57,700

Index

A

B

C

D

E

G

H